*Did You ...*

# SWINDON

## A MISCELLANY

Compiled by Julia Skinner

With particular reference to the work of Brian Bridgeman

# THE FRANCIS FRITH COLLECTION

www.francisfrith.com

Based on a book first published in the United Kingdom in 2006 by The Francis Frith Collection®

This edition published exclusively for Oakridge in 2009 ISBN 978-1-84589-446-7

Text and Design copyright The Francis Frith Collection®
Photographs copyright The Francis Frith Collection® except where indicated.

The Frith® photographs and the Frith® logo are reproduced under licence from
Heritage Photographic Resources Ltd, the owners of the Frith® archive and trademarks.
'The Francis Frith Collection', 'Francis Frith' and 'Frith' are registered trademarks of
Heritage Photographic Resources Ltd.

British Library Cataloguing in Publication Data

Did You Know? Swindon - A Miscellany
Compiled by Julia Skinner
With particular reference to the work of Brian Bridgeman

The Francis Frith Collection
Frith's Barn, Teffont,
Salisbury, Wiltshire SP3 5QP
Tel: +44 (0) 1722 716 376
Email: info@francisfrith.co.uk
www.francisfrith.com

Printed and bound in Singapore

Front Cover: **SWINDON, MEN LEAVING THE GWR WORKS 1913** S254607p
Title Page: **SWINDON, A DECORATED TRAM 1911** S254532

*The colour-tinting is for illustrative purposes only, and is not intended to be historically accurate*

# CONTENTS

# INTRODUCTION

The ever-growing town of Swindon is now Wiltshire's main centre of industry with a population of nearly 200,000, but 200 years ago it was a quiet market town with a population of about 1,200. In the 1830s the Great Western Railway laid its tracks through the fields less than two miles to the north of the old town, and here Isambard Kingdom Brunel and Daniel Gooch established the GWR locomotion workshops, along with housing for the workers, making Swindon a centre for heavy industry and engineering. Some of England's most famous steam engines were made in this factory, and Swindon became known throughout the world as a railway town. The works not only provided the majority of the employment opportunities for Swindon itself for many years, but also for much of the working population of the surrounding area, which was connected to the town by railway and road transport links. The remainder of the inhabitants of the area also depended on the railway to a large extent, providing the essential services and products required by those who worked 'inside' (a local term for those who spent their working lives confined within the walls of the railway works).

By the 1850s the New Town was larger than its old neighbour on the hill. The two towns gradually grew together over the next fifty years, and in January 1900 they joined together as one municipal borough. In due course, Mr G J Churchward, Manager of the Works and later Chief Mechanical Engineer of the GWR, became the first mayor. The population of the town was then around 45,000. The town continued to expand, and in 1928 the borough boundaries were extended by annexation of the whole of the rural parish of Rodbourne Cheney and parts of Stratton St Margaret, so that the whole of the first council housing estate in the area, Pinehurst, came within the borough. Districts that formed parts of other parishes

- Wroughton, Chiseldon, Lydiard Millicent and Lydiard Tregoze - were also included within the new borough boundaries. After the Second World War several large engineering companies came to Swindon or its immediate neighbourhood, including Vickers-Armstrong, the Plessey Company and Pressed Steel Fisher Ltd. These companies also required a large workforce, which stimulated further expansion of the town. 9,000 houses were built within the borough boundary, including the estates of Penhill and Walcot. In 1961 permission was given to build outside the boundary. In 1974 the Highworth Rural District was united with the old Borough of Swindon, and the new authority became the Borough of Thamesdown. Subsequently, further expansion to the west and recently to the north of Swindon has resulted in the incorporation of parts of parishes formerly administered by the Cricklade and Wootton Bassett Rural District Council, and then, from 1974, the North Wiltshire Council. In 1997 the former Thamesdown Borough Council became the new unitary authority known as the Borough of Swindon.

As railway services contracted in the second half of the 20th century, a major rationalisation in the 1980s saw the unthinkable happen, and the Swindon Works closed. But out of adversity came opportunity: the opening of the M4 motorway to the south of Swindon in the early 1970s led to a further expansion in employment opportunities, and the town is now a commercial centre, with computers, finance and the motorcar industry being particularly important.

The story of Swindon is full of fascinating characters and events, of which this book can only provide a brief glimpse.

# WILTSHIRE DIALECT WORDS AND PHRASES

**'A day back agone'** - some time ago, in the past.

**'Cack handed'** - left handed, or clumsy.

**'Chuckypigs'**, **'chuggypigs'** or **'grampfywigs'** - woodlice.

**'Emmet'** - an ant.

**'Gally-bagger'**, or **'gally-crow'** - a scarecrow.

**'Gert'** - big, large.

**'Loppity'** - feeling ill, run-down, under the weather.

**'Nammet'** - the mid-day snack.

**'Narration'** - a fuss, or commotion.

**'Shrammed'**- chilled to the bone.

**'Somewhen'** - some time.

**'Spadgers'** - sparrows.

**'Teg'** - a sheep, thus **'tegman'** - shepherd.

**'Ther thee bist'** - there you are.

**'Vamplets'** - gaiters.

**'Where's it to?'**- where is it?

**'Yertiz'** - here it is.

# HAUNTED SWINDON

Swindon Arts Centre is said to be haunted by a ghostly lady dressed in brown clothes. She has been seen by staff in the bar, sitting at the back of the auditorium and on the stairs. Footsteps have been heard in the building when no one is there, lights have been mysteriously switched on after being switched off, and heavy fire doors have been seen being opened and closed, apparently by an unseen hand.

The Wyvern Theatre in Theatre Square has been the site of several mysterious occurrences. Ghostly black figures have been seen running across the stage and up the stairs, and psychic investigators have reported sudden drops in temperature, seeing strange lights, the feeling of being touched and of hearing strange voices.

The ghost of a woman who was convicted and executed for killing her child is said to roam near St Mary's Church in Rodbourne Cheney, carrying a small baby in her arms.

A ghostly figure is said to stand by the yew tree outside the church of St John the Baptist and St Helen in the village of Wroughton, just south of Swindon. There are several stories about the identity of the figure - one is that it is the ghost of a man who hanged himself from the branches of the tree, but another possibility is that it is the ghost of a woman who was buried in the churchyard, and cannot rest because she died bearing a guilty secret. A tale told by local schoolchildren for many years is that you will see the figure if you run around the tree thirteen times as the church clock is striking midnight.

Lydiard House is said to be haunted by the ghost of Sir John St John. He supported the king during the Civil War, and three of his sons died in the conflict. His ghostly presence is marked by a sudden drop in temperature and a sweet smell in the air.

# SWINDON MISCELLANY

Close by Swindon, the Ridgeway runs along the top of the downland ridge. The Ridgeway is one of the oldest prehistoric trackways in Europe. Evidence suggests that feet may have tramped along this route for up to 5,000 years, and in the 18th and 19th centuries the broad track was used as a droveway, for driving sheep and cattle to distant markets.

Old Swindon stands on a hill which was quarried for stone by the Romans. During the Anglo-Saxon period, there was a small settlement on the hill; the remains of a Saxon sunken house were found behind Lloyds Bank in the High Street, and evidence of Saxon houses has also been found in the area of what is now Saxon Court, behind Market Square.

Swindon is referred to in the Domesday Book as 'Suindune'. The name may be derived from the Anglo-Saxon words for 'swine hill', meaning the place where pigs were kept, or it possibly means 'Sweyn's hill', after the man who owned Swindon Hill in Anglo-Saxon times.

The Richard Jefferies House and Museum at Coate commemorates the life and work of the respected writer and naturalist Richard Jefferies, who was born in the museum building, then a farmhouse, in 1848. He recorded his childhood memories of life in the countryside around mid 19th-century Swindon in a series of novels, most notably 'Bevis - The Story of a Boy'.

**TOWN GARDENS, THE BANDSTAND**
**c1955** S254044

**HIGH STREET, LOOKING NORTH c1950** S254024

The main street of Old Swindon was first recorded in 1581. On the left of photograph S254024 of the High Street, above, stands the Bell Hotel, established, according to the wording over the door, in 1515; it was the departure point for the tri-weekly London coach from Swindon, and was also the post office in the 1830s. The Victorian shop-front of the chemist next to the hotel has now gone - the premises have been taken into an extension and courtyard for the hotel, which has been changed almost beyond recognition in recent years. It is now known as the Fusion restaurant, bar and hotel. The depot of H & G Symonds Ltd (seen further down the road in the photograph) was the former North Wilts Brewery. Later used as an area office by Courage until 1978, the whole site has now been redeveloped as the main local branch of Barclays Bank, although the original façade has been retained.

Woolly mammoths once roamed the Swindon area - in 1998 the skull of a woolly mammoth, approximately 100,000 years old, was discovered by Dr Neville Hollingworth of the Swindon-based National Environment Research Council, in a gravel pit at the Cotswold Water Park between Swindon and Cirencester.

Photograph S254517, below, shows a large crowd that has gathered in Newport Street, part of the Old Town of Swindon, in 1910. The cause of the excitement is not clear, but it could be a fire at the thatched building in the background. The wall of the house on the right is smothered in trade posters and advertisements for the forthcoming attractions at the Empire Theatre.

**NEWPORT STREET 1910** S254517

**MEN LEAVING THE GWR WORKS 1913**  S254607

This photograph shows workers leaving the
Great Western Railway Works, which at one time
employed 14,000 people. The sheer size of the
building indicates the importance of the railway
to the town. The uniformity of dress amongst
the men is striking.

**HIGH STREET, LOOKING SOUTH TO MARLBOROUGH ROAD 1948** S254012

The buildings to the left of photograph S254012, above, stood next to the Old Town Hall on the Market Square. In the 19th century the shop on the corner was a grocer's and baker's owned by the family of the writer Richard Jefferies. The Masons Arms (beyond), with its own stables, which stood opposite the junction with Newport Street, had parts of the building dating back to the late 17th century. Immediately adjacent to this inn in Marlborough Road was another old public house, the Bell & Shoulder of Mutton. This section of the High Street has changed beyond recognition today. Road widening in 1969-70 swept away all the buildings to the left; the HSBC Bank complex, and its adjacent car park, now cover the area.

Wood Street dates back many centuries - the lease of a tenement dated 1599 is the earliest reference. It was also known in the past as Windmill Street (according to the writer Richard Jefferies), after a corn-mill which had once stood here, and also as Blacksmith's Street.

An inn has stood on the site of the Goddard Arms in the High Street for 400 years (see photograph S254014, below). It was known as the Crown until about 1810, when it was renamed in honour of the Goddard family, the lords of the manor of High Swindon. The Magistrates' Court for Swindon was held here until the Old Town Hall was built in the Market Square in 1852. In April 1914 a between-maid here, Frances Priscilla Hunter, was shot dead by her jealous lover, Walter James White. He was executed for the murder at Winchester in June 1914.

**HIGH STREET, THE GODDARD ARMS c1950** S254014

Christ Church, the parish church of the Old Town, was designed by Sir George Gilbert Scott, the eminent Victorian architect, who had previously provided the design for the railway church of St Mark's in the GWR Railway Village; he also designed the Albert Memorial and the St Pancras Hotel in London. Christ Church was built to replace the medieval church of Holy Rood, which was by then too small for the growing population of Old Town. Its tower and broached spire (approximately 150ft in height) are based on the 13th-century church of Buckworth, near Huntingdon, according to John Betjeman, who wrote a poem celebrating the famous peal of bells from this well-loved building on Swindon's skyline, 'On Hearing the Full Peal of Ten Bells from Christ Church, Swindon, Wilts'.

To cater for the cultural needs of the townsfolk, the Corporation of Swindon bought the house and estate of Lydiard Park from Lord Bolingbroke in 1943. This has been developed over the years as a conference centre, a recreation area and a site for large outdoor concerts and Shakespearian productions. The mansion itself, a splendid Classical-style building, was extensively restored and refurbished and opened to the public in 1955. Since then there has been an ongoing programme to find and restore the original furnishings, silver, china, glassware and other artefacts that were in the house during the occupancy of the St John family, who lived in the house from the time of Elizabeth I (Henry St John was created 1st Viscount Bolingbroke in 1712). The picture collection of the 6th Viscount Bolingbroke was also purchased by Swindon Corporation for permanent display in the house.

CHRIST CHURCH 1948 S254018

**THE GWR STATION 1905** S254509

When the New Town was established around the railway works in the mid 19th century, other facilities besides housing were provided for the workers and their families. A church (St Mark's) and a school were also built with funds subscribed by shareholders of the railway company. In addition, some enlightened welfare projects were set up by the GWR, including a Medical Fund Society to provide medical and other care for the railwaymen and their families, which in many ways anticipated the Welfare State of today.

**FLEET STREET c1955** S254026

At one time Swindon was a distribution centre for Wiltshire's well-organised and widespread smuggling trade. In 1874 the Revd A C Smith described how in the 18th and 19th centuries smuggling was the main source of employment for many villages on the north Wiltshire Downs and around Swindon; the area had good communication links to other smuggling communities on Salisbury Plain and the Dorset and Hampshire coasts, and much

use was made of ancient trackways in the area. Beneath many houses, cottages and inns of Swindon were tunnels and cellars where contraband brandy, tobacco, lace and such-like were stored before being transported to illicit markets further north. Smuggling has been romanticised in folklore, fiction and film, but was often a vicious and violent trade, full of intimidation and corruption in high places.

**SWINDON, HIGH STREET 1915** S254524

19

**REGENT CIRCUS AND REGENT STREET**
**c1950** S254021

Swindon was the scene of a riot in 1919, when its councillors decided to pay £200 to erect a 50ft flag pole with a gilded top-piece outside the Town Hall as part of the peace celebrations at the end of the First World War. The townspeople felt that the money could be better spent providing help for ex-servicemen, and the flag pole was burnt down by protestors; the following day feelings were still running high, and the remaining portion of the pole was used to smash shop windows in Regent Street.

At the centre of photograph S254021, opposite, stands Swindon's Cenotaph. This replaced a temporary wooden structure that was erected after the flag pole riot (see above) and was unveiled in October 1920 to commemorate the fallen of the First World War.

In the background of photograph S254021, opposite, the view is dominated by the giant Classical-style portico of the Baptist Tabernacle. This impressive structure was designed by W H Read and opened in 1886; it cost £6,000 and had seating for 1,000. Constructed of Bath stone, the colonnade of six Tuscan columns supported a large pediment. The building was demolished in 1978, and the site was bare until the new Pilgrim Centre was constructed and opened in 1990.

Ian Fleming, the creator of James Bond, 007, is buried in St James's churchyard in the village of Sevenhampton, a few miles from Swindon.

Swindon's motor industry is often overshadowed by the town's railway heritage, but it has been a major employer in the area ever since Pressed Steel Fisher Ltd came to the town in the 1950s. The company has gone through several takeovers and changes of name, but is now Swindon Pressings Ltd (SPL), owned by BMW, which manufactures car body plant. The company makes parts for BMW's New MINIs, which are assembled in Oxford. The Honda plant at South Marston began production of cars in 1992, and Honda is now the town's second biggest employer. Honda Accords, CRVs and Civics are models that have been built in Swindon. The millionth Swindon-built Honda car was produced in 2003. The importance of the motor industry to Swindon was recognised in 1997, when the coat of arms of the Borough of Swindon was updated - the swan sitting on the top of the coat of arms is resting one of its feet on a car wheel.

Swindon is famous - and notorious - for a traffic system known as 'the Magic Roundabout', although its original name was the County Ground Roundabout. The Magic Roundabout became its official name in the late 1990s, since this was what everyone called it! Constructed in 1972, the roundabout consists of one large roundabout incorporating 5 mini-roundabouts within it. Traffic flow around the larger roundabout is counter-clockwise, but the traffic around the 5 mini-roundabouts and the outer loop flows in a clockwise direction. The system inspired a song, 'English Roundabout', by the Swindon band XTC.

THE TRAM CENTRE c1919 S254518

**QUEEN'S PARK c1955** S254069

Queen's Park was laid out in the centre of Swindon,
close to Regent Circus and the Town Hall, using funds
donated for the coronation celebrations of 1953. The man
credited with creating the park from a former claypit and
area of derelict land is Maurice Williams, who was the
General Superintendent of Parks from 1949 to 1975. He is
commemorated with a plaque on the wall at the entrance
to the Garden of Remembrance off Groundwell Road; the
wording on the plaque echoes the inscription over the tomb
of Sir Christopher Wren in London's St Paul's Cathedral: 'If you
would see his monument, look around'.

Photograph S254535, below, was taken on 10 September 1961, the last day of passenger services on the former Midland & South Western Junction Railway line that connected Andoversford (near Cheltenham) to Andover and the south. The station, opened in 1881, was situated off Newport Street near the junction with Devizes Road. The M&SWJR was taken over by the Great Western Railway under the Railways Act of 1923. During both World Wars this vitally important strategic route carried an immense amount of military traffic north and south. After the Second World War, however, traffic reduced, and the line was closed along with many other country routes. The photograph shows the Railway Correspondence & Travel Society Tour train in the station - one of two special trains that ran that day over the line for the benefit of railway enthusiasts. Today the site of the station is the Central Trading Estate, with light industrial units, and the route of the line between the station and west Swindon is a pleasant cycle and pedestrian path.

**SWINDON TOWN STATION 1961** S254535

Coate Water was originally constructed in 1821-22 as a reservoir, and was designed to overcome water shortages on the canal system around the town after the North Wilts Canal opened in 1819. In 1914 Swindon Borough Council purchased both Coate Water and sections of disused canal within the town. Since this time, it has been built up to be a major attraction for local people.

The concrete diving stage seen in photograph S254036, below, was officially opened at a gala in June 1935. One of the celebrities giving a demonstration on this occasion was Miss Cicely Cousins, who had won the ASA High Diving Championship in 1934. Sad to say, the structure has not been used since swimming here was stopped, owing to pollution of the lake.

**COATE WATER, LOOKING WEST TO THE DIVING BOARD c1955** S254036

**TOWN GARDENS, THE BANDSTAND AND THE REFRESHMENT KIOSK
c1955** S254039

**TOWN GARDENS, THE CONCERT BOWL OPEN-AIR THEATRE 1948** S254017

The Town Gardens were laid out in the late 19th century on the site of old stone quarries formerly owned by the Goddard family. These quarries had given Swindon an important industry long before the arrival of the GWR, for the stone was considered of excellent quality. In 1893 the Old Swindon Local Board purchased the quarries, and the gardens were opened in May 1894 by Mr W Reynolds, Chairman of the Board.

After the Great Fire of London in 1666, stone from Swindon's quarries was in great demand for paving the newly built streets of London.

The small octagonal building of the refreshment kiosk in Town Gardens, seen to the extreme right of photograph S254039, opposite, has an interesting history. It was built in the GWR Works in 1914 to be used as an advertising trade stand, and appeared in many large agricultural shows and other exhibitions all over the country - it was easy to erect and could be carried in a normal railway wagon. In 1942, after lying unused for many years in the GWR stores, it was purchased by the Borough Council and erected in the Town Gardens as a café.

The Art-Deco Concert Bowl in Town Gardens is situated in a valley that was the former main quarry area (see photograph S254017, opposite). It is one of only a handful built in this country in this style. In the 1990s the Concert Bowl was restored with the support of Burmah Castrol plc, and is now the venue for regular summer concerts and drama productions.

**REGENT STREET 1948** S254009

Regent Street, seen in photograph S254009, above, was
originally lined with workers' cottages, but from about 1865
many of these dwellings were converted into shops. The small
shop fronts to the left of the photograph were built out from
the original terraced houses. On the far left of the photograph
is the Regent Street Primitive Methodist Church; it had been
built to replace two former chapels on the same site, of 1849
and 1863. In 1895 a large Sunday school was built behind the
chapel. This building remained in use even after the chapel
itself was demolished in 1957, and served for many years as
Swindon's first arts centre and as the children's library.

*Did You Know?*
# SWINDON
A MISCELLANY

In the centre background of photograph S254009, opposite, is William McIlroy's store, with its ornate clock tower, which was a landmark in this part of Swindon for many years. It was a complete shopping experience for generations of Swindonians. The store had an elegant stairway between the ground and first floors, which was said to have come from an ocean liner. The clock tower and the Edwardian frontage were demolished during refurbishment of the store c1960, but later some attempt was made to reintroduce the period look to the store windows. However, the store closed in the 1990s, and the whole area was redeveloped as separate units. A new clock tower was built in 1999.

**REGENT STREET c1965** S254065

**REGENT CIRCUS 1902** S254523

The name of Highworth Warneford School in Swindon
commemorates a local hero from the First World War,
Rex Warneford (his family owned Warneford Place in
Sevenhampton), a lieutenant in the RNAS, who shot down a
Graf Zeppelin over Brussels in 1915. When Lt Warneford first
tried to attack the Zeppelin in his plane he was driven away by
its defensive machine gun fire; he climbed to 13,000ft and then
bombed the Zeppelin from above. His plane was damaged in
the subsequent explosion and he had to make a forced landing
behind enemy lines, where he managed to make emergency
repairs before taking off for the safety of his airbase. Lt
Warneford was awarded the Victoria Cross for his bravery, but
tragically he was killed ten days later.

*Did You Know?*
# SWINDON
A MISCELLANY

The building shown in photograph S254090, below, was originally built by the Great Western Railway as a lodging house for single men in 1846, and was called The Barracks. It was converted to a chapel for the Wesleyan Methodists by T S Lansdown of Swindon in 1869, and could accommodate a congregation of 1,000. Closed c1959, it became Swindon's Railway Museum in 1962 and remained as such until 1999. The new Steam Museum was opened in 2000, and the old Railway Museum building is now used by the New Mechanics' Institution Preservation Trust in their quest to restore this area of Swindon's railway heritage.

**THE RAILWAY MUSEUM, FARINGDON ROAD c1965** S254090

33

'History starts yesterday' is the motto of the Swindon Society, which records the social history of the Swindon area. The Society has amassed a large collection of slides and photographs which illustrates all aspects of life in the changing town since the mid 19th century, and helped fund the purchase of a number of negatives and prints by the local photographer Albert Beaney

**REGENT STREET c1965** S254064

which are held in the Swindon Museum and Art Gallery. The Society has produced a number of books showing Swindon in old photographs, and was also able to provide an early photograph of the windmill at Chiseldon from its collection, which helped when the windmill was moved and reconstructed as the centrepiece of the Windmill Hill Business Park.

A new railway museum, 'Steam', to celebrate the GWR Works and the men and women who worked there, opened in 2000. The museum is housed in a restored Grade II railway building on Kemble Drive, in the heart of the former Swindon Works. The whole story of locomotive manufacture, the building of the GWR and its history is told here in fascinating detail in various forms, including rare archive film footage, memories of ex-railway workers, hands-on exhibits, interactive displays and railway memorabilia. Around the museum are life-size figures of railway staff, many of them modelled on real people who worked for the GWR, and the Wall of Names chronicles the men and women who were employed at the Swindon Works. You can even have a go on a simulator to get a feel of what it was like to drive a steam engine.

**GWR TRIP, SWINDON WORKS 1910** S254601

**BROAD HINTON, THE WHITE HORSE c1955** B377003

Photograph B377003, above, shows the hill figure cut in the chalk on the face of Hackpen Hill, to the right of the road from Wootton Bassett to Marlborough. It is believed to have been cut in 1838 by Henry Eatwell, parish clerk of Broad Hinton, assisted, according to some accounts, by the local publican, to commemorate the coronation of Queen Victoria. It is approximately 90ft square in size.

In the Steam Museum is Isambard Kingdom Brunel's walking stick, which can be seen near his statue. This walking stick unfolded to make a measuring stick that was exactly 7ft long, and could be used to check that the broad gauge lines of the GWR track had been laid correctly.

In its heyday the Swindon Works produced three locomotives a week, but at some cost - for instance, the noise of the Boiler Shop meant that most of the workers there had become deaf by the age of 30. An account of the working conditions was published in 1915 by Alfred Williams, known as 'The Hammerman Poet', who worked

**FLEET STREET 1913** S254608

there from 1892 until 1914. 'Life in a Railway Factory' was acclaimed by the critics, and The Times reviewer praised the work, saying 'This book may be read either as pure literature or as a social study; it is both'. However, the GWR magazine condemned the book, and unfortunately it did not sell well in the Swindon area.

# SWINDON
## A MISCELLANY

Swindon is the setting for the popular 'Thursday Next' series of novels by Jasper Fforde, although it is a Swindon in a rather surreal parallel universe, similar but quirkily different. In an interview Jasper Fforde said that he decided to set the books in Swindon because it struck him as a place where anything could happen: 'I'm very much promoting an alternative sort of Swindon. You can actually come here and see what my alternative Swindon would look like but you have to sort of screw up your eyes slightly…The similarities are the layout … all the road layouts and everything are the same … the differences with my Swindon and Nextian Swindon, as I call it, is that it has an underground system for instance. It has a monorail system, it's very, very modern and lots of things go on there.' It has been suggested that at some time in the future parts of Swindon might be named after characters in the books, such as Braxton Hicks, Bowden Cable, Thursday Next, and Penzler Pick. In the meantime, take a hilarious look at Jasper's view of the Seven Wonders of Swindon on his web site, www.jasperfforde.com/swindon/7wonders.html

**WOOD STREET c1950** S254022

# SPORTING SWINDON

Swindon Town Football Club had an extraordinary start in the Football League. After joining Division Three South as one of the founder members in 1920 the club won its first match, against Luton Town, by 9-1. This remains the club's highest ever win in the League. Swindon Town's history was to be a little less eventful over the next 40 years. The club spent every season from 1920 to 1958 in the same division. The club only moved division when the League was reorganised, and Swindon Town joined the new national Division Three.

The most famous match in Swindon Town Football Club's history is of course the 1969 League Cup victory over Arsenal at Wembley. It was the club's finest moment, and in retrospect seems even more incredible, as Arsenal were to win the League and FA Cup 'Double' just two years later. However, the club has been involved in a number of other notable games. In 1911, Town played against Barnsley in Paris for the Dubonnet Cup. It was a game played between the two losing FA Cup semi-finalists. Swindon won the match at Parc des Princes, beating Barnsley 2-1 to bring the trophy home. This was no mean feat, as the trophy weighed nearly a hundredweight! In the same year, Swindon played against Manchester United for the Charity Shield. It was the highest scoring Charity Shield match, Swindon sadly losing 8-4.

Swindon Town player John Trollope still holds the record for the most Football League appearances for one club. He played 770 times for Swindon in the League between 1960 and 1980.

Swindon was the birthplace of one of Britain's greatest jockeys. National Hunt jockey John Francome was born in the town in 1952. He won over 1,000 races during his illustrious career, and was Champion Jump Jockey seven times. One major triumph to evade him was winning the Grand National, his best result being a second place. John Francome was awarded the MBE in 1986, and has written a string of best-selling novels set in the racing world.

# QUIZ QUESTIONS

Answers on page 48.

1.  The name 'The Old Lady on the Hill' refers to what?

2.  Who is commemorated in the name of Fleming Way?

3.  What was the affectionate name given to the GWR - the Great Western Railway?

4.  Where in Swindon can you find Caerphilly Castle, and what is it?

5.  What is the connection between Swindon and the Bayeux Tapestry which depicts the Norman Conquest of 1066?

6.  The famous hooter of the Swindon Railway Works blew for the last time on 26 March 1986. For over a century this had sounded over the town to call thousands of people to work, but it was disliked by the 5th Viscount Bolingbroke of Lydiard House - why was this?

7.  Swindon's motto is 'Salubritas et Industria' - what does this mean?

8.  Swindon is twinned with which three places in the world?

9.  A recent award-winning novel was set in Swindon. What was it?

10. Locations in Swindon have been used in two James Bond films - where were they, and which films did they feature in?

**DEVIZES ROAD 1908** S254513

**REGENT STREET c1913** S254519

# RECIPE

## WILTSHIRE MARKET DAY DINNER

**Ingredients**

6 pork chops
2 pig's kidneys, sliced
450g/1lb onions, peeled and
sliced

1 apple
1 teaspoonful chopped sage
Salt and pepper
450g/1lb potatoes
150ml/¼ pint water or stock

Put the chops into an ovenproof casserole. Cover with the sliced kidneys and onions. Peel, core and slice the apple and put on top. Sprinkle on the sage, and season well with salt and pepper. Peel and slice the potatoes and cover the top of the dish with them. Pour on 150ml/¼ pint water or stock, cover and cook at 170 degrees C/325 degrees F/Gas Mark 3 for about three hours.

**QUEEN'S PARK c1965** S254068

**THE TOWN HALL c1965**  S254086

# RECIPE

## WILTSHIRE FAIRINGS
*Fairings are small, spicy, crunchy biscuits that were commonly sold at fairs.*

### Ingredients

225g/8oz self-raising flour
1½ teaspoonfuls bicarbonate of soda
A pinch of salt
1 teaspoonful ground mixed spice

1 teaspoonful ground ginger
½ teaspoonful ground cinnamon
110g/4oz butter
50g/2oz sugar
110g/4oz golden syrup

Sift the flour, bicarbonate of soda, salt and spices together, and mix well. Rub in the butter until the mixture resembles fine breadcrumbs, then add the sugar and mix well. Warm the golden syrup a little, then pour it into the mixture, and knead it until it has formed a firm dough. Flour your hands, then roll small amounts of the dough into balls about the size of an egg, and put the balls onto a greased baking tray, well spaced out. Flatten each ball down well with the back of a spoon. Bake at 190 degrees C/375 degrees F/Gas Mark 5 for about 10 minutes, or until golden brown. Remove from the oven and cool on a wire rack.

# QUIZ ANSWERS

1. Christ Church, the parish church of the Old Town.

2. Fleming Way is named after Harold Fleming, the footballer who played for Swindon Town from 1907-24, and who was capped for England eleven times.

3. The GWR was affectionately known as 'God's Wonderful Railway'.

4. The 'Caerphilly Castle' can be found in the Steam Museum in Kemble Drive, and is a magnificent example of the locomotives that were once built at the Swindon Works. It is displayed in pristine glory in 'ex-works' condition, with gleaming brass and paintwork.

5. After the Norman Conquest of 1066, Swindon was given to King William's half-brother, Bishop Odo of Bayeux. It was Bishop Odo who commissioned the Bayeux Tapestry to be made.

6. The Viscount complained that the noise disturbed the pheasants sitting on their eggs on his land. In his book 'A Swindon Retrospect: 1855-1930', Frederick Large describes the reaction of the workers to this complaint: 'So bitter were the GWR employees and hundreds of others not employed in the Works, that a petition miles in length (it was said at the time) was signed and sent to the proper quarter objecting to his Lordship's action, which had the desired effect'. The hooter no longer blows, but its domes still stand above the entrance of what is now the McArthur Glen Designer Outlet (a shopping complex built within the old Swindon Works).

7.  Swindon's motto 'Salubritas et Industria' means 'Health and Industry'.

8.  Swindon is twinned with Ocotal in Nicaragua, Salzgitter in Germany and Torun in Poland.

9.  'The Curious Incident of the Dog in the Night-time', by Mark Haddon, which won the 2003 Whitbread Book of the Year award.

10. The former Renault building (now known as the Spectrum building) in West Swindon was used in 'A View to a Kill' (1985), and the modernistic Motorola production plant in Abbey Meads featured in 'The World Is Not Enough' (1999).

**THE GARDEN OF REMEMBRANCE, GROUNDWELL ROAD c1955** S254049

**REGENT STREET c1955** S254029

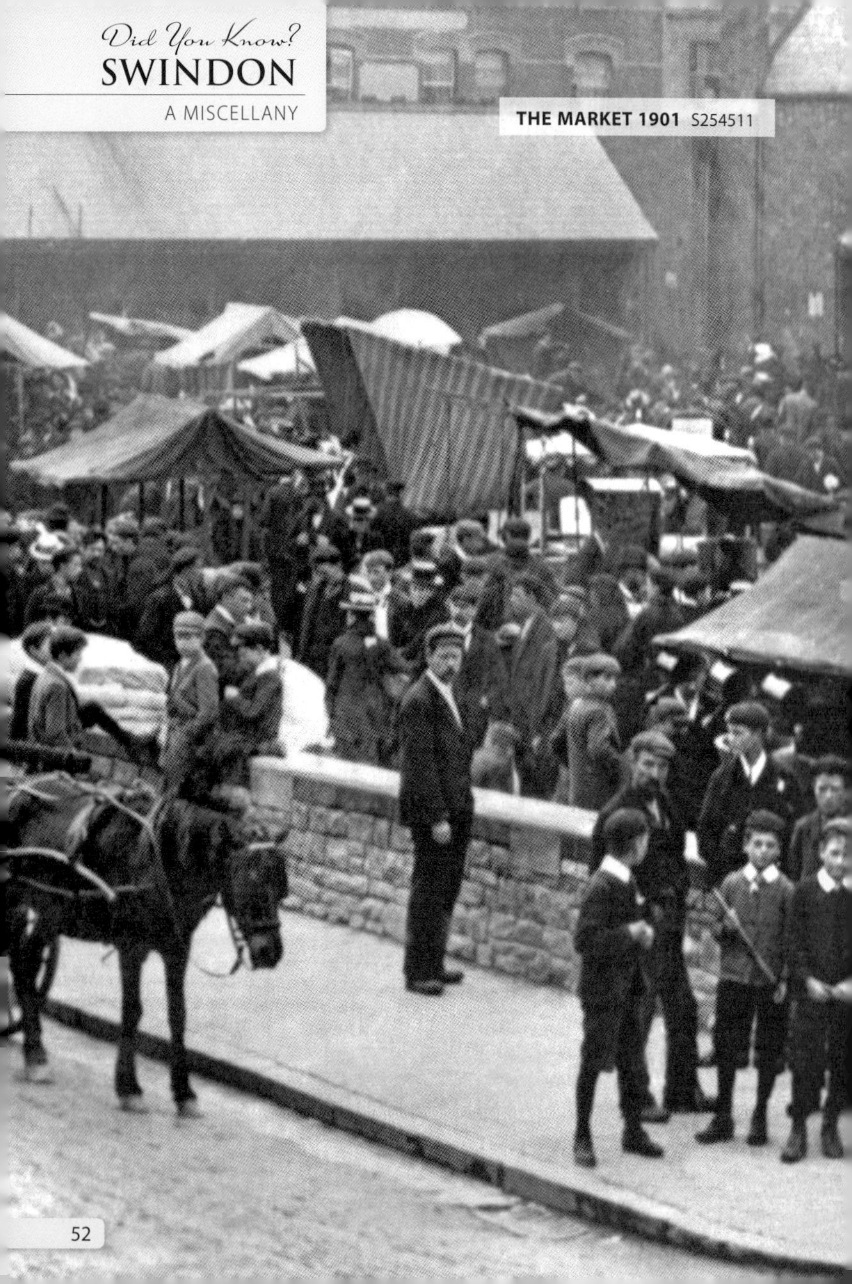

THE MARKET 1901 S254511

# FRANCIS FRITH

## PIONEER VICTORIAN PHOTOGRAPHER

Francis Frith, founder of the world-famous photographic archive, was a complex and multi-talented man. A devout Quaker and a highly successful Victorian businessman, he was philosophical by nature and pioneering in outlook. By 1855 he had already established a wholesale grocery business in Liverpool, and sold it for the astonishing sum of £200,000, which is the equivalent today of over £15,000,000. Now in his thirties, and captivated by the new science of photography, Frith set out on a series of pioneering journeys up the Nile and to the Near East.

## INTRIGUE AND EXPLORATION

He was the first photographer to venture beyond the sixth cataract of the Nile. Africa was still the mysterious 'Dark Continent', and Stanley and Livingstone's historic meeting was a decade into the future. The conditions for picture taking confound belief. He laboured for hours in his wicker dark-room in the sweltering heat of the desert, while the volatile chemicals fizzed dangerously in their trays. Back in London he exhibited his photographs and was 'rapturously cheered' by members of the Royal Society. His reputation as a photographer was made overnight.

## VENTURE OF A LIFE-TIME

By the 1870s the railways had threaded their way across the country, and Bank Holidays and half-day Saturdays had been made obligatory by Act of Parliament. All of a sudden the working man and his family were able to enjoy days out, take holidays, and see a little more of the world.

With typical business acumen, Francis Frith foresaw that these new tourists would enjoy having souvenirs to commemorate their days out. For the next thirty years he travelled the country by train and by pony and trap, producing fine photographs of seaside resorts and beauty spots that were keenly bought by millions of Victorians. These prints were painstakingly pasted into family albums and pored over during the dark nights of winter, rekindling precious memories of summer excursions. Frith's studio was soon supplying retail shops all over the country, and by 1890 F Frith & Co had become the greatest specialist photographic publishing company in the world, with over 2,000 sales outlets, and pioneered the picture postcard.

## FRANCIS FRITH'S LEGACY

Francis Frith had died in 1898 at his villa in Cannes, his great project still growing. By 1970 the archive he created contained over a third of a million pictures showing 7,000 British towns and villages.

Frith's legacy to us today is of immense significance and value, for the magnificent archive of evocative photographs he created provides a unique record of change in the cities, towns and villages throughout Britain over a century and more. Frith and his fellow studio photographers revisited locations many times down the years to update their views, compiling for us an enthralling and colourful pageant of British life and character.

We are fortunate that Frith was dedicated to recording the minutiae of everyday life. For it is this sheer wealth of visual data, the painstaking chronicle of changes in dress, transport, street layouts, buildings, housing and landscape that captivates us so much today, offering us a powerful link with the past and with the lives of our ancestors.

Computers have now made it possible for Frith's many thousands of images to be accessed almost instantly. The archive offers every one of us an opportunity to examine the places where we and our families have lived and worked down the years. Its images, depicting our shared past, are now bringing pleasure and enlightenment to millions around the world a century and more after his death.

For further information visit: www.francisfrith.com

## INTERIOR DECORATION

Frith's photographs can be seen framed and as giant wall murals in thousands of pubs, restaurants, hotels, banks, retail stores and other public buildings throughout Britain. These provide interesting and attractive décor, generating strong local interest and acting as a powerful reminder of gentler days in our increasingly busy and frenetic world.

## FRITH PRODUCTS

All Frith photographs are available as prints and posters in a variety of different sizes and styles. In the UK we also offer a range of other gift and stationery products illustrated with Frith photographs, although many of these are not available for delivery outside the UK – see our web site for more information on the products available for delivery in your country.

## THE INTERNET

Over 100,000 photographs of Britain can be viewed and purchased on the Frith web site. The web site also includes memories and reminiscences contributed by our customers, who have personal knowledge of localities and of the people and properties depicted in Frith photographs. If you wish to learn more about a specific town or village you may find these reminiscences fascinating to browse. Why not add your own comments if you think they would be of interest to others? See **www.francisfrith.com**

## PLEASE HELP US BRING FRITH'S PHOTOGRAPHS TO LIFE

Our authors do their best to recount the history of the places they write about. They give insights into how particular towns and villages developed, they describe the architecture of streets and buildings, and they discuss the lives of famous people who lived there. But however knowledgeable our authors are, the story they tell is necessarily incomplete.

Frith's photographs are so much more than plain historical documents. They are living proofs of the flow of human life down the generations. They show real people at real moments in history; and each of those people is the son or daughter of someone, the brother or sister, aunt or uncle, grandfather or grandmother of someone else. All of them lived, worked and played in the streets depicted in Frith's photographs.

We would be grateful if you would give us your insights into the places shown in our photographs: the streets and buildings, the shops, businesses and industries. Post your memories of life in those streets on the Frith website: what it was like growing up there, who ran the local shop and what shopping was like years ago; if your workplace is shown tell us about your working day and what the building is used for now. Read other visitors' memories and reconnect with your shared local history and heritage. With your help more and more Frith photographs can be brought to life, and vital memories preserved for posterity, and for the benefit of historians in the future.

Wherever possible, we will try to include some of your comments in future editions of our books. Moreover, if you spot errors in dates, titles or other facts, please let us know, because our archive records are not always completely accurate—they rely on 140 years of human endeavour and hand-compiled records. You can email us using the contact form on the website.

Thank you!

For further information, trade, or author enquiries please contact us at the address below:

**The Francis Frith Collection, Frith's Barn, Teffont, Salisbury, Wiltshire, England SP3 5QP.**

Tel: +44 (0)1722 716 376  Fax: +44 (0)1722 716 881

e-mail: sales@francisfrith.co.uk  **www.francisfrith.com**